TOP **10** REASONS WHY YOU MUST WRITE A BOOK

DINESH VERMA

Published Internationally by

Pendown Press
Powered by Gullybaba.com

PENDOWN PRESS

Powered by **Gullybaba Publishing House Pvt. Ltd.,**
An ISO 9001 & ISO 14001 certified Co.,
Regd. Office: 2525/193, 1st Floor, Onkar Nagar-A, Tri Nagar,
Delhi-110035, (From Kanhaiya Nagar Metro Station Towards
Old Bus Stand)
Branch Office: 1A/2A, 20, Hari Sadan, Ansari Road,
Daryaganj, New Delhi-110002
Ph.: 09350849407, 011-27387998
E-mail: info@pendownpress.com
Website: PendownPress.com

First Edition: 2020

Price: ₹199/-

ISBN: 978-93-89601-55-8

Layout Design: Pendown Press Publishing

LIST OF CONTENTS

Thank you for opening this book. I am sure, you will end up becoming the author of your insta-book (or book) of international standard in just 7 days by breaking all your barriers that are putting hurdles in your willingness to becoming the author of an insta-book having compelling content and killer design. The insta-book that you will be authoring very soon will serve a number of purposes, such as making the dream of becoming an author, arousing inquisitiveness for your profile among your readers, the business that you do, the workshops that you organise, or the motivational speech that you deliver and most importantly, carving a niche for yourself in the society, to share the important message with society, all these contribute to the masses and to you as an author. I will be describing "how" later in this book.

I know you are very excited to know about the methodologies of writing. Do you want to be aware of MM Methodology which will lead your potential clients get attracted towards you and the existing ones to stick with you forever? Do you want to magnify your magnetism?

I know your answer is A BIG YES.

I will introduce you with this MM Methodology very soon.

ACKNOWLEDGEMENTS

I owe a profound sense of gratitude towards everyone I have interacted with regarding publishing, especially those who started their journey and published their book with Pendown or any publishing company. I am delighted to see them becoming a Published Author.

It makes me happy beyond words when readers send feedback about the impact of our books in their life. A big thank to all those readers from the bottom of my heart.

Last, but not least, the Almighty, the Superpower which is superior to everything, the very power which made me a medium to pendown few words, which may impact Millions of Lives.

INTRODUCTION

As a Publisher and author, I am frequently asked for advice on dealing with authoring a book, using book to build credibility and authority. Having supported hundreds of Entrepreneurs, Coaches, Professors, Trainers, etc. become Published Author, I am delighted to have a chance to grow the book publishing with the mission to create 10,000 authors, thereby impacting 10 Million lives on this planet by 2025. I am really thankful to the Almighty, and all those who have helped me make my Gullybaba Publishing House Pvt. Ltd. the Largest and No.1 Company in IGNOU Self-Help Books in the World.

23 years back when I took admission in MCA through IGNOU, I noticed that the Study Material given by University for MCA through correspondence, was not sufficient. Even Google Baba was not that knowledgeable. We had very limited access to computer; finding a knowledgeable teacher was then a herculean task as well. I could see all these difficulties on the face of fellow students. Deep inside me, I used to think, "What can I do to overcome all these challenges?" I started thinking:

Ohhh... this is really a big market to serve where people don't have right support material.

From that need and pain, my journey started. I prepared notes and started to distribute them to my fellow mates which became a blessing in disguise. To the best of my knowledge, it clicked. My friends and I really did well in examination. This was shocking to me like anything. What's happening here!!! I couldn't believe it. I continued to prepare notes with all the enthusiasm... Soon that excitement came to an end as all the money that I had, got spent.

I had no money left even to photocopy and circulate the notes. In 1997, I opted for home tuitions and made some money. Then students requested me to start charging them for notes but DON'T STOP. After this I decided to publish my notes as a Book. This was BY FAR one of the scariest decisions of my life. I published my First book, named "computer fundamentals". Forget about people, I was myself not able to imagine this big achievement of my life.

I still remember the days when I used to paste posters on the walls of universities early morning so that nobody can notice me and catch me. Sometimes I had to use the word STAFF to avoid ticket while commuting through public transport, as I had to save every single rupee that I had.

I am in gratitude towards GOD and the universe for showing me the path to serve my society. My eyes always looked for the people who believed in writing, gaining freedom, generating business around books, but not knowing the HOW of becoming an author. I had good reason to help them because they cared for their society and had a message to share.

I have a lot of love and respect towards the real building blocks of society, i.e., Entrepreneurs, speakers, coaches, trainers and consultants, who trusted me to serve them by building their personal brand through books and cementing them as The Authority in their industry/area of activity.

After running Gullybaba successfully for almost two decades, I started toying with the idea of having an exclusive platform for entrepreneurs, Coaches, Speakers, consultants for the greater good of the society. And in this way Pendown Press was conceptualized. I am quite happy and thankful to the Almighty that Pendown Press is now ready to function on full swing.

Pendown Press is a global platform for all those who have something to share to the world, and believe in the impact of books on the business and millions of lives. We help you build a concept, write, publish, and market your book to influence the world and supercharge the marketing. In the last few years, we have redefined publishing for the greater benefits thereby enabling writers to start their Star-studded journey to become an influential authority by writing & publishing bestseller book in no time so that they can benefit quickly, which means more Income and Impact.

Backed by our parent company (Gullybaba) started on 13th October, 2000 as a provider of online notes on computing, today, Pendown Press is created to serve the real building blocks of our society primarily. That aims to answer-- What to write?, How to write?, How to print? I cannot write. How can I grow my business through books? Etc... to steering authors to the finish line, thereby making them publish their books internationally.

Till today, we have published 1500+ books in total, which covers fiction & non-fiction topics. I have worked with senior scientists, authors in India, UK, Dubai, and Ukraine. Many of our Authors have got selected by GOI for Beijing, South Africa, Landon, UAE, and other International Fairs in their official catalog for respective countries. I got a chance to meet the President of India Honourable Shri Pranab Mukherjee in Rashtrapati Bhawan in the year 2014 to gift a book on the environment published by my publishing house.

What motivate me are transformational testimonials, smile on the faces of readers, authors and shopkeepers. When everybody earns their living and engaged making this world a better place to live in, nothing could be better than this

A book is what took me and my business to the next level, which was exactly the reason why I wrote each one. That's why here I am with my website BestsellerWithDinesh.com where I want people to take the insta-book out in 7 days' time. Millions of people in India would like to take their book published, but because they don't know how to publish their books in very short span of time, they struggle. In fact, they do not put adequate effort to make their dream see the light of the day.

However, it is important to note here that Insta Book should not be the norm of writing, like Glucose, or any energy booster should not be the only intake. These things cannot replace a proper meal.

You should opt for Insta-Book as the foremost strategy to enter into the publishing world. Insta-Book is evergreen. You will find it beneficial every day and in every situation. It is a sure-fire way if you want to get your book published within 7 days. As and when you get feedback on your insta-book you can go for writing a full-length book. It is what you go for.

WHAT IS AN INSTA BOOK?

I s Insta Book the Next Avatar of Book?

Is Insta Book a Need in Today's Digitalised Era?

Is Insta book the first milestone to be touched during your journey to write a bestseller book?

I know your excitement level might be at all-time high. You might have started feeling tempted to know about Insta Book. But, before I remove curtain, I would like to tell you about the background which became the foundation of my brainchild, i.e. insta Book.

I meet lots of people, among them there are entrepreneurs, coaches, speakers and trainers. Many of them tell me that they want to write book. Some even go to the extent of saying that they have been thinking to write book from last 10 years, 5 years or something similar kind of thing. Some says, they will publish book even in their 5th meeting with me. There is surprising element as well, because their confidence level tends to be the same for several months (rather, years in some cases), without writing even a single page, or any miniature picture of how their book-to-be will look, the title it will have, its readers, whether it will be a mini book, or a voluminous one.

It is not that they lack on anything—be it the topics, the knowledge required, the willingness to do something for the greater good of the society, or the money required. And when all these people start coming on the screen of my mind, when I feel relaxed, I tend to get upset.

I start conversing with myself, "How Come! Are not they making their society deprived by not doing the things they are immensely capable of? Have they made their pre-conceived notion (that book writing is more difficult than all the difficult things put together) so powerful that it overshadows all the power that they possess.

I keep on telling them—you are already a writer, you have written very good comment in my Facebook page, your blog is so impressive, your vocabulary is richer than so many established authors, your LinkedIn article suggests that the only reason you are not becoming author is because you yourself do not want to, so on and so forth.

I suggest some of them to write just a book with only 30 pages, which will be very consumable. Here, by easy consumable I mean, a book which can be read within a few hours and which can benefit readers almost instantly.

When I was telling all these things to the brother of one of my friends from Dubai, he innocently said, "*Bhai*

Saheb, I want to write a book, I do not want to make energy drink, which will provide instant energy to my readers.

His answer was indeed very interesting. I burst into laughter. And from there, I coined the term Insta Book. After that, I worked on this concept. I did also create "hour glass template of book writing" which made it easier further.

When I started clearing the idea of Insta Book to them, they started feeling confident and excited. Now book writing became easy for them.

My idea is to bring out as many as authors as possible, as everyone has something unique to share to this world.

My idea is to break the long-standing belief in the minds of people that book writing, publishing and launching is a big task and they cannot do, due to so many reasons.

Every reason is myth, only reason is not taking first step which is to pick pen and start writing.

Moreover, in today's scenario everyone is busy and have time constraint. It becomes easy for the people to read or consume Insta Book. It's not about writing 30 pages and getting them printed by local printer. It's much more than that. To bring authority through books, there is a certain way you need to do it. And I have been guiding people about it. So many entrepreneurs ask me, "Is there a way where I can write content in my way and you get it done by experts?" I tell them that this is very much possible. Because you are not professional writer, you are just idea giver. Once you write your ideas, tips, technique, or story, it's the job of experts to bring it out in a way that readers become compelled to buy your product or services.

WALK THE TALK WITH ASPIRING AUTHOR

I was in an evening party thrown by one of my author Mr Deepak Sharma, whose book Move Mountain has become the Amazon Best Seller and is touching new level of popularity with each passing day. Mr Deepak had invited me to have an informal conversation in that evening before he left for US.

There were so many august persons there. It was my high privilege to get the opportunity to spend some quality time with some dignified and impressive personalities. In that meeting, I started talking to a gentleman who was sitting next to me in a round table arrangement. There were 3-4 people more with this gentleman.

There was one Entrepreneur, two Public Speakers, one Coach running a wellness company and one a good student of philosophy. Dr. Veda was also there. The entrepreneur was the first person I talked with. He became candid very soon: I am an entrepreneur. I cannot put my hands in so many businesses. I have however good idea on "What type of business" is good for "what kind of people", "What kind of business will bring benefits in small amount of period" so on and so forth, but I am still dreaming for the day when people will listen to me, clients will confide on me, my business will prosper on my personality, so on and so forth.

Soon, a public speaker intervened...

I am already motivating people and making them take actions to grow individually as well as financially. But, I am struggling to have more participants; I want to serve more than 100 participants together in every workshop of mine.

The conversation got another Twist of Talk. A public speaker who was few shows wonders, started talking further, "Mine case is little bit difficult. I had few successful seminars on NLP (Neuro Linguistic Programming_) in recent past. But, perhaps the people's perception has changed drastically these days. Lots of seminars are there in market, so how can I differentiate or stand out in such a crowded market? I need to invest more than INR 2000 to 3000 to get one participant to my free introductory workshops. Approx 50 comes every time, but there remains very low conversion rate, when it comes to registering participants to higher ticket size product or services. Though I am planning a three-day long workshop in September this year, but I know its fate already.

My new friend who was running a wellness company then started telling his own Sordid Saga: I think you people have been telling about my own life. This is exactly what has been happening with me guys. After attending so many seminars and failing to draw the audience, I felt as if no one wants to be healthy, they all want to be wealthy, wealthy and only wealthy, nothing else.

Now, it was the turn of a good student of philosophy. He started telling, "I think it is better not to try my luck on addressing people. Since I am a student of philosophy and there are still good number of people in India who want to listen to Philosophy Fundas, I was toying with the idea of conversing with large number of audience on various seminars. But, No... Now onwards I will try something else.

Dr. Sharma too had his part of problem. He slowly but eloquently started telling, "I am also fed up with telling my patients what to do what not to. I think my voice carries no wait. I wish I could become an authority in my field so that my suggestions get take well care of. But, I think I am demanding too much with my patients.

Till that moment I was keeping quiet, listening to them with rapt attention. But, it was my turn to come into picture. I almost abruptly quipped, "Hey...you all may have different kinds of ailments. But one medicine will cure all your problems.

"Aiiii, they all spoke in Chorus with glitter in their eyes.

Yes, you read me right. I am not joking. It will bring more clients, authority, credibility control over clients, bring down negotiation for my Entrepreneur friend, whereas my friend who is trying his luck as an NLP coach, will get audience and my hitherto ordinarily impressive motivational speaker will see surge in the number of audience he has been getting till now. Likewise, my Philosophical Friend will also be able to spellbind his Audience...

And yes, my frustrated wellness company related friend will get success as well. Likewise, Doctor Sharma will too get authority and his voice will spell magic to patients. Along with the authority, he will also get more and more number of patients.

And, most importantly, all these will be available in almost no time and with lesser amount of money that you spend for digital marketing. You all will be able to sky-rocket your position.

But, what is this? Again it was like a Chorus.

Now, it was the time to announce...

Launch Your Book...

And Book is the Strong Foundation for using the MM Methodology.

MM Methodology & Pain Points

MMM is an acronym that stands for *Marketing Magnetism Methodology* which contains arsenal to attack all the barriers which stops your potential clients to get attracted to you, converted, and finally become your client making you flourish and prosper.

One of the important components of MM Methodology is giving "Leave behind Material" to the client/participants so that they can recall, remember you for longer period of time and refer your name.

MMM speaks through the minds of the prospective readers by living up to their highest expectations and catering to their needs and requirements appreciably, effectively and brilliantly. Honestly telling, it does not do any kind of marketing, what it does is mind reading and creates lasting impressions. The prospective clients themselves do the remaining things.

Attention: People Buy from People

MM Methodology can work wonders for you, irrespective of the industry you are in, provided it is put together in a seamless and cohesive manner.

The very first step towards this Methodology is to have an *insta-book* or a book in your name, targeted to your potential clients. Your *insta-book* is like your first release on a Dolby Screen. It is going to bring stardom for you. Finally, you become haunted instead of you hunting for clients.

Trust me, I speak of my Experience.

(I am writing about this at length in my book "Do not Die With A Book Inside You")

After displaying a miniature picture about MM Methodology in front of you, I will like to explain you about the Pain Points of Entrepreneurs, Speakers, Intrapreneurs, Coaches, Consultants and The Common People, etc.

The Pain Points

1. Entrepreneurs

- How you will become Authority in the industry you are in?

- How you will get an edge over your competitors?
- Will the impact over their clients be short-lived or Permanent?
- Not getting leads or potential clients
- More negotiation during client meetings
- Big potential clients not giving meeting time easily
- Tired of visiting networking seminars/organisations; lots of time get wasted with unsatisfactory results
- Not perceived as an expert
- Struggling to be taken seriously.
- Building a support network.
- Balancing business and family life.
- Coping with a fear of failure.
- Social Capital:
- Finding the First Users.
- Being Rejected from Investors.
- Getting and Keeping Talent.
- Competitors who are low in knowledge and competence, supplying inferior quality product, but quote higher prices than yours.

2. Speakers

- Why will people hear to me?
- What if I plan a Seminar and get compelled to address an empty seminar?
- Not perceived as an authority in my industry
- Less conversion to higher price product or service
- People ask too much questions
- Their contribution towards their society is moving at a snail's pace
- Someone keeps interrupting you.

3. Intrapreneurs

Who are Intrapreneurs?

Though you will not find this word in a dictionary, but it is very common in business world. An intrapreneur is the one who is toying with the idea of entering into business; though he or she is still in a job.

- Why my potential clients will trust me as I am new in this industry?
- How will I build my credibility among already-crowded market?
- How will I grab my potential clients' attention towards me?

- Not getting leads or potential clients
- More negotiation during client meetings
- Big potential clients not giving meeting time easily
- Tired of visiting networking seminars/organisations; lots of time get wasted with unsatisfactory results
- Not perceived as an expert

4. Coaches/Consultants

- How to charge higher?
- Not asking for higher prices due to fear of losing clients?
- And some are common which are already listed
- Getting initial clients and a steady flow of leads
- Scaling their coaching practice towards 6-figure levels
- Moving beyond fees into information products/ online
- Biggest challenge is how to change the mindset of the people in an environment that is not that open to change
- Specifically for Coaches: The biggest challenges have already been mention, but I also find having clients understand the difference between coaching and consulting can be a challenge. They often just

want ideas/suggestions rather than learn how to effectively find those answers for themselves.

5. Any Tom, Dick and Harry

I have no portfolio, why should people listen to me? Though it is good, I know, but I have doubt I will be able to convince my people through conversation. If I fail to get good number of people in my initial days of addressing people, it

BREAK YOUR BARRIERS

What keeps you away from writing your bestseller book? Maybe you have one (or all) of the following excuses as barriers in becoming bestselling Author:

- "I am not a writer."
- "I do not know how to write a book."
- "I am too young (or too old) to write a book."
- "I do not know anyone from the publishing industry."
- "No one knows me."
- "I am too busy to write a book."
- "I do not have money to publish a book."

    Or, the list could be even longer than what I have provided...

I will however like to talk about some most common myths that I have noticed in most of the people whom I have interacted with, in the last two decades:

1. A book cannot bring profit for my business

Reality: A book may or may not bring profit. If it is written to roar in the market; there can be no reason why the book will not bring business and its author will not get name and fame. Forget book, even the cover page can create magic.

From years of experience Gullybaba Publication House has devised IIC Protocol for the cover page of its books. The acronym IIC stands for Impact Integrate Compel. We design the cover pages of our books following this protocol. I will just like to quote a person who just glanced over the cover page of one of our books. Here is what she said:

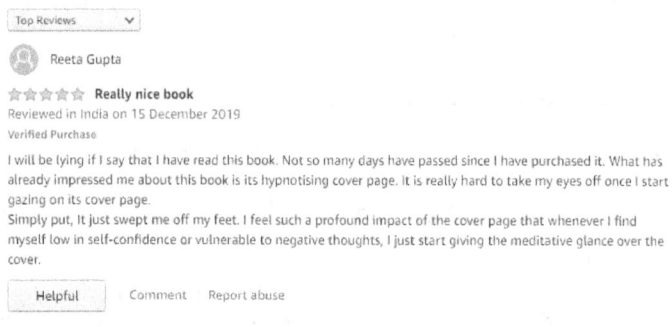

From Amazon.in

For Hindi Translation of Move Mountain book

https://www.amazon.in/Paane-Chaah-Parvat-Denge-Raah/dp/B07RRXWZJ5

Second Case Study

The CEO of Dialdesk, Mr. Deepak Kashyap, Author of Junoon-Jugaad-Jarurat, used his book cover to establish authority and that created magic. His Book cover launched in International Book Fair, 2020, Jan, in Pragati Maidan, New Delhi. He got recognitions, appreciations through the launch and he has been able to make big impact on prospects and clients as well.

> **TIP: Use your book to wear your CAP 2.0 which will explode the lead box for you.**

2. Book will not Bring Authority

Reality: This is another big myth associated with the entrepreneurs. Let's visualize about a moment: Let's Welcome Entrepreneur and Author of......" following your name; you are automatically taken more seriously than any other candidate who is just described as an "Entrepreneur." By now, you might have understood as to how book will bring authority to you.

How about getting introduced you in seminars or other leading events like Author ABC is going to address us within next two minutes...Being Author brings more respect and accolades for you. Audience will be responding to your words with more thunderous clapping, could your prospective clients be able to prevent themselves from buying your words and buying the products that you sell or seek the services that you provide?

How about sending book with hypnotic cover letter? You will become Authority for him as soon as he sees your book and reads that cover letter.

This technique has earned commands for all those authors who have adopted this. It has enabled the authors to control their conversation with clients, assert their authority, and make their clients agreed on their own terms (high charge).

You will serve them best and they will welcome your products or services like a farmer does when he perceives that a monsoon rain is about to fall.

Mr Sanjay Kumar, Real Estate Demand Generation Expert authored two books for different set of clients and became able to start his coaching business from 1-2-1 to 1 to Many, and has been able to grow his business multi-fold.

> **TIP: Use your book to enter JVM (Joint Virtual Machine) which will bring you cooked leads leading to more business almost automatically.**

3. Reading Books is not necessary to avail my products/services

Reality: If you are also among those entrepreneurs who entertain any such kinds of feelings, you need to give a re-look to your thought. Mind, any client of yours who purchase your products or avail your services, does a number of things apart from fetching services from you. If you are able to speak through the minds of your prospective clients through your book, there will be many things they will like in your book, and their admiration for your book will turn into availing your services.

And even if he does not read your book at all, he will have some kind of picture about you in his mind, and that some kind is basically the picture of yours as an Authority or Expert. There are many real case studies about manufacturers.

Chetan Jain is an Electronics Engineer from Bharti Vidyapeeth College of Engineering, Pune and MBA from NMIMS, Mumbai. He is an entrepreneur involved in the manufacturing of shrink sleeves, BOP wrap on labels and flexible laminates. He authored insta-book to increase profits by optimising shrink sleeves requirement. It is for Indian FMCG companies who are using shrink sleeves and who intend to use them for their product containers, bottles, jars & cups made of all kinds of materials.

> **Everybody wants to do business with Authority or Expert.**

4. I am a business guy. Even 24 hours is not enough, how can I write?

Reality: This is one of the most common reasons that are cited by entrepreneurs as an excuse for not writing a book. Mind, Phil Knight, the creator of Nike, shoes and/or an athletic brand had same time as you have. Nonetheless, he wrote a book Shoe Dog: A Memoir by Phil Knight. Therefore, stop making excuses and start writing.

Importantly, book writing does not involve so much of time. You can better start with thin book having 100-120 pages max. Mind, you do not have to serve big content to your readers; all that you need to do is to establish your credibility and for that thin book will suffice. With the help of my Hour Glass Approach, you can write 100 pages' book by spending mere one hour daily.

...In my full length book... I will share the templates which can make your book's outline draft out in one day.

Mr. Vinod K Pandita, could author his book in 16 hrs time, The Powerful CeO. which has won high regards from his clients and converted prospects into clients easily.

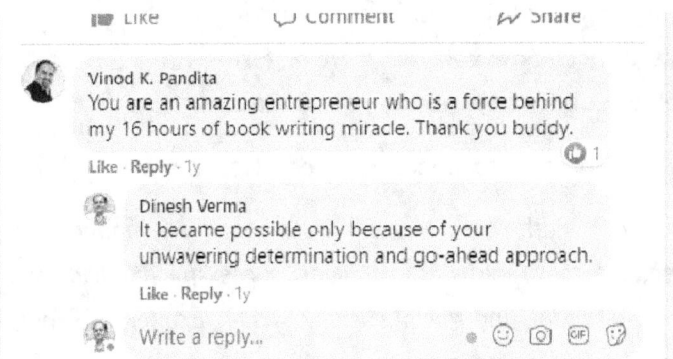

Above is the comment by him on my Facebook.

> **TIP: You can Transform Your Life in no Time: Do booklet instead of book.** It takes total of only 7 days— right from thinking about business generating topic, to writing the contents, cover design, and publishing by Traditional Publisher. Yes, I mean it. The total time required is 3 hrs to 7 hrs maximum. It's incredible, but true.

5. I need to be an expert

Think about an expert, says a great cricketer, hollywood or bollywood star, a subject expert, speaker, etc. Have they all become expert first and then done their first movie, first match, first class, etc.? I think by now you might have understood the fact that your book will earn the position of expert for you and in order to write a book, you need not be an expert.

Moreover, you need not write a full-length book in first effort. You can very well start with a booklet and make people know about your potential.

Write book to become a perceived Expert.

Vivek Pathak, authored insta-book on finance "From Mediocre to Wealthy" he is highly successful financial planner and consultant and got published by HT, Economic Times and other prestigious newspapers.

6. I need to be good in writing

Most of the people take language of books so seriously that they cite their linguistic inferiority as the main reason for not writing a book. I have come across several persons, though fairly competent and knowledgeable to write books, bowing their head in the name of book writing in the pretext of Linguistic Lack. What a Pity!

Reality: As a writer, your only job is to visualize and conceptualise a book. The rest will be taken care by the people, who are adept at doing these things. Take an example of Film Making. Do you think an actor or actress does the entire things related with movie making? If you believe, they do not; you will be convinced of writing a book, even if you are not a linguistically superior person. Make your first draft of book in less than 5 hours through

Book Mind Mapping and give it to expert content developer, then to the editor for editing.

You need to follow systems and templates. It's a science of getting book ready in 7 days & on the shelf & online platforms like Amazon/Flipkart within 7 days. See yourself how it is getting sold on these platforms.

- **Prisms of Life**

  Dr. Roopinder Dogra had very poignant and inspirational story to tell. But, she was dithering to share it. I am thankful to the Almighty for I convinced her to write the book and rest is history. After this book, she came with another book (Perception's).

7. The topic of my book needs to be different & unique

So many aspiring authors tend to be topic-driven. They keep on exploring for their topic for months, may be because they are under the impression that if their topic becomes unique, the book will be a resounding hit, no matter whether they write in the underneath pages or leave it blank. They think that there are already so many books existing in market on the same topic. Then who will buy my book? Why people will read my book?

Reality: If your book is on common topic, it's a good thing! It means it's a popular topic that is why so many people are writing on this topic. Mind, information needs to be unique, not the topic alone. If the content of your book is unique, informative, though-provoking, solution-giver, there is no reason why the audience will not jostle to take your book.

India's #1 Business Clarity Coach, Amit Chawla coaches CXO's, Sr. Executives, Entrepreneurs and Business Owners. He became a resounding success after publishing his book "The Clarity First". He was facing the similar challenge. Pendown legal and editorial team's support successfully got him overcome this myth from all the perspectives.

8. People will read my book, only when I am famous!

Reality: If you are the one who entertains these types of thinking, you are probably missing a great chance to become famous. In most of the cases, its contrary is correct. That means, you become famous when you write a book.

Take example of Napolean Hill's famous book Think and Grow Rich. You will get amused to know that he himself became rich (famous) after giving the concept that mere thinking can create richness.

- **Father Builds, Son Kills**

  This book mentions 9 Great Ways to Build a Scalable and Profitable Business Which can Run Without You. The book became talk among the business people and soon lots of other businesspersons came ahead to publish book through us.

9. Writing a book will not make me any money!

If you think that book will not beget money, you have probably not seen or heard of billionaires created by books.

Take example of J.K. Rowling of Harry Potter series. She thought of writing a book on a delayed train from Manchester to London in 1990.

Still I suggest you to write with the intent of building business around book instead of writing with the intent of earning by selling books.

Of course, you would want to earn more clients, more business instead of having intent of earning 50 to 100 bucks by selling books. It does not mean that I am against earning through book selling, of course selling would always be there, but energy will be focused towards getting more clients through books.

- **Fix your knees without a stitch**

  The popularity of Dr. Pankaj Bharti, the author of this book soared after his book "Fix your knees without a stitch" published with us. People knew about his knowledge and the ability to treat joint pain in unconventional and effective ways through this book.

Book selling is not your primary earning source. Stay Focused, Earn High. Focus on to earn a client who pays in lakhs, instead of a book buyer who pays you just 200-500 bucks

---

I can shake off everything as I write; my sorrows disappear, my courage is reborn—Anne Frank

---

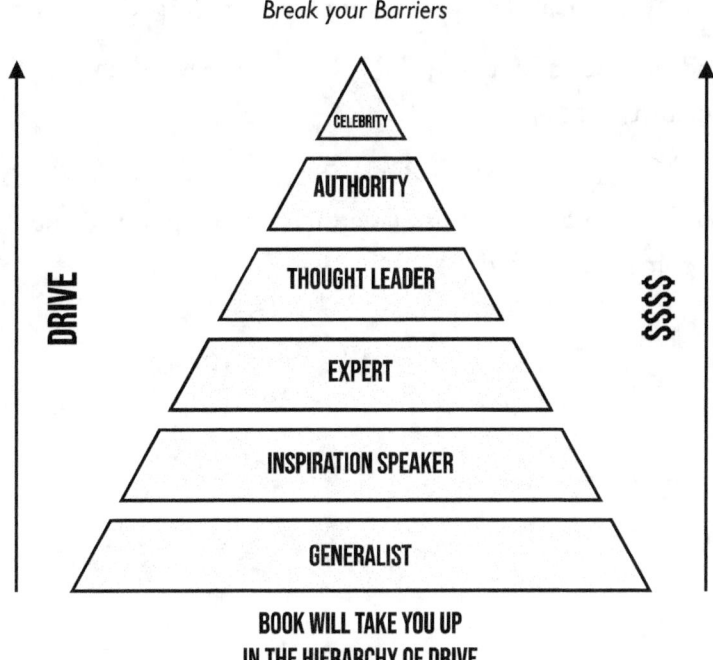

DRIVE

$$$$

CELEBRITY

AUTHORITY

THOUGHT LEADER

EXPERT

INSPIRATION SPEAKER

GENERALIST

**BOOK WILL TAKE YOU UP
IN THE HIERARCHY OF DRIVE**

Authority +

See the illustration about what I call the hierarchy of derive. I'm probably not the first to present this idea, and I believe there is magic in a book for almost anyone looking to grow a business, and explode their income and impact.

The concept of the hierarchy of desire is that as your sale ability increases in the eyes of your ideal client, so does your attractiveness and your charge. The magic is in how your book propels you from generalist or even specialist to expert, and eventually to a Leader/Authority

23

and if you adopt the MM Methodology, then to the celebrity status.

As I say often at Pendown Press, as you scale up in the hierarchy, you get transformed from hunting for clients to become the hunted.

LOOK FOR WHY

Let's put yourself on Fire to Publish Book

Before delving deep into writing, publishing and marketing of your book, define the purpose of beginning this journey. It is simply because if you become able to define your purpose very well, everything will start falling soon in sequence and the way you want this to happen.

Whenever people approach me for writing book and start flooding me with their lofty ideas, I tend to ask them: What is your purpose? What are your objectives? Where do you want to go with this project?

Whenever my above-given questions are replied with a blank stare or the answer, "The only thing that I know is I have to write a book and I think there is nothing more I should be knowing about" it sounds really fun. Though with all humility, but I do insist them to explore their Purpose First.

May be your answer will be, "What reasons should I tell you and what should I hide. There are truck loads of reasons why I want to write a book. I am writing because so many else are writing, or I want my readers to enjoy reading my book. Or, it's on my to-do list.

I am sorry, but those answers are far from being apt.

Why

It is simply because all these are reasons, not the purposes. When you get the purpose, it will not let you relax even for a moment. Rather, it will keep you hooked with your book and get you write from start to finish, almost in one go(If you are planning to authoring insta-book, which is the right way).

Choose the End to Start

Begin with the end in mind.

–The second habit in **Stephen Covey's Seven Habits of Highly Effective People**

Taking a common theme in the creative process, we are going to start at the end and work backwards, an approach called "PR (Plan-Reverse)."

That's why I ask people in the beginning "What your book launch date is?"

If you are among those potential authors who take "becoming a published author" quite seriously, it's the time to start thinking like an author. The first thing that is needed to be done in the book-writing mindset is to determine the end goal of your book.

Spare some thoughts about it. What level of success do you want for yourself and your book?

You may be willing to become an Amazon bestseller, get a thousand leads for your business, or sell five hundred copies of a book YOU published.

You do not want to remain Underpaid, Underestimated, or Undervalued? Right...

Do you want to charge higher?

Do you want to be perceived as an expert?

Your competitor is having lesser expertise and still doing better than you, and you have decided to be THE Authority in your industry.

Do you want to stay away from the crowd?

Do you want to have the borrowed credibility by interviewing Authorities or experts in your industry?

Your Clear Answer of the BIG question WHY will set your book in your hand before your next client meet.

10 REASONS WHY YOU SHOULD WRITE A BOOK?

1. Adding Author before your name itself creates better perception about you

2. Makes Passive income; you are getting paid for it forever by just working on it once

3. Creates Dream Business and Inspires others to live better lives

4. Become Amazon Bestseller Author

   Thousands leads for your business, Looking for Perfect way of capturing leads.

5. You are no longer Underpaid, Underestimated, and Undervalued

6. You qualify to Charge Higher

7. You want to be perceived as an Expert

8. Writing book stamps your authority. You become Authority Figure in your Field and you get the reason why your competitor is doing better than

you, despite having lesser expertise and knowledge than you have

9. You stand away from the crowd

10. Book helps you expand your own network by creating a good story, talking about a passion project

Apart from the above-given reasons, there are some more reasons why you should write a book. These are as follows:

1. You can put Writer in your designation

2. Great revenue generator for your business

3. It will build your reputation. Mind, having no reputation at all is just as bad as having a bad reputation

4. Book to your credit will gain credibility in your field or create creativity in a new field. Book will help you explain as to how you could emerge as a successful and worthy of conversing with such a large number of people

5. Your book becomes like a Mover & Shaker in your business

6. Your book works as your physical presence on the desk, bag, shelf, etc. of your audience. The book

makes them think of you, reminds about you and drive them to contact you

7. Book is a great way to connect with influencers like authors, journalists, podcasters and bloggers who are competent enough to grow your network. Resultantly, it saves your time spent on networking events

8. Having best-seller in your name will increase your magnetism; people will keep on getting connected with you almost naturally

9. If you have just entered in a particular field or planning to enter, then it will help to even the playing field between you and the experienced ones, making you respectable from the start

10. The last and most important reason is "Because you always had a desire to write". But, your desire remains suppressed in the absence of a coach, who could have made the journey of book publishing smooth.

CRAFTING YOUR CRAFT

Creating multiple bestseller books, one for every product or service in your funnel. Certainly, it will elevate you in the *hierarchy of brand*. From no brand to attaining celebrity status and becoming a brand face in the industry through bestseller books, you will have a general understanding.

Now, let's discuss a few things which can make your book a Bestseller. Once you are clear about your audience by answering few questions, you can proceed further to work upon your Craft i.e., your Book.

1. Laying the Bestseller Foundation

It is a herculean task to mark your presence in bestseller club. If not strong then you will end up with tag of a Bubble Book *i.e.* a book failing to impress the audience. Very soon the reader would lose enthusiasm. I come across with many who start their book and leave in midway or just after launching it. But we always educate them and suggest them to take necessary instructions from publishing team. When team and author work in unison, things become easier and taking baby steps at the appropriate time, leave you with another bestseller in your name.

As you have read this book, I am giving you this template as Token of Appreciation. This template is a magical template which will make you clear about your potential clients and tell you to get your book out only for your potential clients or clients, to establish your authority in your industry, and not just another book which will not do anything for you and which will not transform your life or business in any way. Publishing book happens to be the first potent weapon in the arsenal of MM Methodology (Marketing Magnetism Methodology).

Now, I acknowledge that you might already have your book done or might be well on your way to finish it. What I ask is that you try to leave some of your preconceived ideas about the topic of your book at the door, so that we can discover together a truly solid foundation for your work.

To lay a solid foundation for your book, I'd like you to answer 7 simple questions. Answering them would lead to a clarified mind, which will be more actionable than a thinking mind. **Once you get the answer for all seven, you can mail me at publishmybookdinesh@gullybaba.com or Whatsapp the pics. at: 8130886000**

1. Write all the specific goals or desired outcome that you have/wish for your book.

    _____

    _____

    _____

    _____

    _____

    _____

    _____

    _____

    _____

2. What is your audience's main problem or concern that you can solve by writing this book?

    _____

    _____

    _____

    _____

    _____

_____

_____

_____

_____

3. What is the conversation going on in the readers' heads, so that you can hook them?

_____

_____

_____

_____

_____

_____

_____

_____

_____

Or

What are the "broken record" conversations that you have with client or prospect?

_____

_____

_____

_____

_____

_____

_____

_____

_____

4. What do you get paid for your expertise?

_____

_____

_____

_____

_____

_____

_____

_____

_____

5. What are you most passionate about/a topic you know a lot about?

_____

_____

_____

_____

_____

_____

_____

_____

6. What is your favourite hobby?

_____

_____

_____

_____

_____

_____

_____

_____

_____

7. What kind of people (designation, age group, profession, etc.) come to you for advice?

_____

_____

_____

_____

_____

_____

_____

_____

_____

2. Crafting your Bestseller Title

Books are judged and sold on covers and titles. Approach this topic lightly at your own (and your book's) risk.

Before you craft your bestseller title, I would like to educate you about the cover and title of a book briefly.

Use this space to write down all of the potential book titles you've already thought of:

_____

_____

_____

_____

_____

_____

_____

_____

_____

_____

_____

Crafting Your Title

There are 3 primary characteristics of a good book title

A good book title should be:

1. Curiosity-provoking/Compelling

2. Interesting

3. Memorable

Another key element of many successful book titles is that they're *short and sweet.* Finding a word or short phrase for your topic and audience is like diamond. If you can find one, two, or three words that **have the ability to capture your readers' mind,** and it creates curiosity or emotion, then your arrow is on the target.

Some examples of titles that are both short and curiosity-provoking include:

Malcolm Glad well's national bestselling books, Outliers, Blink, and The Tipping Point.

And few others by other authors are GRIT, Angela, Move Mountains

Crafting your title is crucial to the success of your book. Take the time necessary to get it right!

Nature of the bestseller book title is that **it hooks the audience.**

The book title gets the target group to *connect with the book*. It creates a need to read it by building a perception. Title works on the philosophy of *"sell them what they want"* and *"give them what they need"* through the content. It should be based on the want not on the need of the consumer or reader. The book title needs to be a combination of Left brain (logic) and Right brain (creative).

Always remember: **The Title is Vital.**

Use the space below to make your earlier titles more curiosity-provoking, interesting, memorable, and clearly expressed.

_____

_____

_____

_____

_____

_____

_____

_____

_____

Crafting Your Subtitle

If your title is short, curiosity-provoking, like the one we have discussed above, then it will almost certainly need a subtitle to give further explanation and benefit to the reader. The subtitle of your book is your descriptive, benefit-rich wordings that explain the **Crux of the Content** of your book.

Types of Titles

Giving Shock

Stop Chasing Customers, Construct Building in Just 60 Seconds

Controversy

What They Don't Teach You at Harvard Business School

Borrowed Credibility

Awaken the Rockstar Within (Inspired by "Awaken the Giant Within" Authored by Tony Robbins)

Asking Question

How to Manufacture Time? By Chandan Goyal

Humour

The Naughty Story of Building For Free, How Not To Hate Your Husband after Kids

I usually ask our authors to avoid Direct (Safest and Boring Theme) as these types of titles leaves least Amount of Impact on audience.

Below, I am giving examples of titles of my upcoming book. You will get more clarity about how you can craft your Bestseller Title.

Direct: How To Publish Your Book

Shock: Publish Book Before You Die / Get Published Before You Die

Question: How To Publish Book In No Time? / Who Will Praise You When You Die?

Bold: Don't Die With A Book Inside You

Curiosity: My 1st Imperfect Book / This Book Has Lots Of Mistakes.

Finally, I selected the BOLD one: *"Don't Die With A Book Inside You"*.

A book is always judged by its cover.

3. Endorsements

Have you ever noticed that all the Bestseller Books have GREAT Endorsements? Have you ever wondered why and how? What is the importance of BIG and GREAT Endorsements? If you're an aspiring Bestselling Author, read the next few paragraphs very carefully!

Endorsements add legitimacy to a book. It is like an added promotional material when someone picks up your book. Moreover, you can put your endorsement to optimum use by putting it in the free samples of your book available for your online readers. Rest assured, it will hook your readers and make them hanker after your book.

After knowing the importance of having an endorsement for your book, you need to know as to **who can write endorsements for your book.** One simple answer to this question could be: **The Influencer or Role Model to your Target Group.** Simply put, if your book is on education, your target reader is students, teachers, etc. So, in that case, a respectable name in the education sector could be the ideal person and you can approach them to write an endorsement for your book. Likewise, if your book is on film, a big name in the film industry will be the ideal person for writing endorsement. One of the books published at my publishing house, *Effective Parenting,* got endorsed by Tisca Chopra, the lead actor of the movie

Taare Zameen Par. Her endorsement gave a great message to the society, as besides being a popular star, Tisca is also a parent.

Contrary to what so many aspiring Bestseller Authors of today think, getting endorsement for your book from big names is not difficult. You may feel that way, too. In fact, it is a win-win situation for both of you. If you get good exposure to your book because of that person, he or she also gets more name and fame through your book. For anyone, the name in a book is a more effective advertisement than that of a newspaper. In fact, you can also get **endorsement in the form of Book Review by the prominent newspapers.** Moreover, who will not want to get associated with knowledge? However, if you want to be on the safer side, make a list of 10 persons, who you think are appropriate for writing you an endorsement.

At Knopf, we look at each book on a case-by-case basis... in some cases, we think a writer might get a boost from an endorsement by a fellow writer, but in other cases, a new book will be better served by other means, such as publicity and reviews.

Sonny Mehta, Chairman
Knopf Doubleday Publishing Group

The only thing that you need to take into consideration is **how you can make this endorsement writing easy for the person** that you intend to get an endorsement from. If you take good care of his or her engagements, possibly *you could write something* and send him or her in the format that person likes, like PDF, Print, WhatsApp Message, Google Keep, etc. for approval, the entire work of getting endorsement can prove to be a cakewalk.

Subtitle is very direct specific explanation of what the book is about.

4. Back Cover

Back cover is very important to make your Authority; you can always declare future of your industry at the back, which we do with our authors in 121(One-to-One) with them. It helps projecting them as the Authority. One day over dinner with Sam Cow thorn in Surya Hotel, Defence Colony, we were discussing its importance. He said, "It's a one liner which can shift your audience's mind towards you in positive way."

Back cover is also important because whenever readers visit stores or online store, they browse for all the pictures of your book before buying. If your back cover is attractive and having all the ingredients of good back cover, then it will also support you in making your book a bestseller.

We have seen lacks of visitors coming to International Book Fair, and we see so many pics of the book by its cover, then they also check the back cover.

Back is Important.

Elements of a Good Book Back Cover: Your quote. Always remember => Your quote, you quote.

- Brief Description about the book. What reader get, objective of book.

- Brief description about the author.

- Testimonials and Endorsements.

- Publisher details and References

- ISBN with Barcode

The back cover needs to sell the book!

5. Reviewed By Reputed Newspaper Or Magazine

Sending book to good newspapers and magazines is a prudent choice, but I know they receive so many books daily. And they mostly avoid publishing reviews of self-published books. For that we always suggest authors to sign C-Contract with publishers thereby giving them leverage for the book. Though only a few self-published books becomes bestsellers through this technique, but if you have designed your press release in a way, or editor likes your concept ...there are chances that will get some presence in their newspaper.

When our book e.g. HOW TO HAVE VICTORY got reviewed by Dainik Jagran in Nov., 2019 the book touched bestseller chart instantly. Its author will be enjoying the bestseller title for the rest of his life.

Single strategy can make you earn the bestseller title. And once you touch that chart, you can always enjoy bestseller title in front of your name.

6. Launch your Launch Team before Bestseller Book

Use a Launch Team to Spread Your

Message with Velocity and Create your Next Bestseller

In this marketing phase, it's not just techniques and information that

You'll need to succeed, but also a little oomph.

Mukesh Kulothia confessed, though, that when he reached the marketing phase, he was feeling stressed:

The most intimidating part of my publishing was by far the launch.

I didn't know how to get people on my launch team. I didn't know how to get people buy my book. That's where these simple steps saved the day. I didn't have any excuses. I had an outline. All that I had to do was to accomplish each daily task and trust the system.

Just as Mukesh admitted, when it comes to marketing and launching your book, it is quite natural to feel intimidated. Many first-time authors feel this way. It's a big transition stepping out of the mindset of creative and into the mindset of selling.

This is one of the most important reasons why creating a launch team is a must. The team members that you have hand-picked, will prove to be of great help and benefit during the book launch. They will make sure that the launch of your book is a huge hit. Simply put, they will be like your right hand. You, along with your robust team, will be able to host a stellar launch.

Once Mukesh created launch team through our "5 Steps Launch Team Creation." His book soon touched the bestseller chart. He became so excited with the phenomenal success of his book, that he launched the Hindi section of his book too. Now, he is engaged writing his third book with us, which is on leadership.

Intro about Launch Team

Your launch team should be efficient and effective enough to multiply your magnetism, calm down your stress, expand your reach, magnify your skills, and above all capable and competent enough to depend on you.

Now,

Who are these radioactive people? What is the mechanism of their support? Why would they lay their hands on your venture? Let's start with all these important questions:

"Who" Your Dream (Bestseller) Launch Team

The "Who" of your bestseller will comprise the people who either care about you, or the message/story that your book carries. However, it is not impossible to find the people who can fulfil in both these criteria.

If you are toying with the thought of who will be in your launch team, you can count on the people in your innermost circle, and the people connected with them. Mind, the people who really care about you, will definitely care about the message that your book conveys. They will be able to churn out Marketing Mantra out of your book, that might spell magic to your targeted readers. The people in your innermost circle could be your spouse, siblings, children, cousins, in-laws, best friends, best friends' children or siblings, colleagues, colleagues' spouses, colleagues' family or friends, neighbours, and neighbours' friends and family.

"HOW" To Get Benefit

The people you select in your team will not stick to "busy work" tasks. Rather, they will be intelligent enough to utilize every single opportunity for the greater good of your book. They will work on marketing tactics to make your book flourish.

They will be

Using their social media to make the presence of your book felt in large audience

Putting positive book reviews on Amazon that will pave the way of popularity of your book

Downloading your book from Amazon, even if they've received a PDF of it

Considering who would benefit from your book, and make your book reach to them

Contacting through blogs, magazines, newspapers, sites about new books, podcasts, YouTube channels or personalities, and Twitter personalities that either would be interested in your Book, or gain attention from your ideal audience and ultimately become your buyers.

Contacting the people at local levels who might be interested in your book. For example, local educationists, businesspersons, leaders, people from political circles, eminent religious leaders, columnists, heads of NGOs, sportspersons, owner of schools, colleges, temple, church, club, mosque, etc.

Establishing a Amazon.com Author page about you and your book.

Hope I gave you fair enough idea. I know there are lots of other stuff with regard to launch team like 5 Steps to create Awesome Launch Team, and Call Scripts and How to approach them, and Milestones and more…I will discuss most of the concepts in more details in my upcoming book "Don't Die With A Book Inside You."

WHY 2020 IS THE BEST TIME TO LAUNCH YOUR BEST SELLER?

Because it's a Low-touch Economy: We cannot deny the fact that Corona has created chaotic situation across the globe. It has created the era of gloomy economy, which the economists of today predict, will not die down in the next 2 to 3 years. Recently, Delhi Chief Minister has also said that we will have to learn with Corona. For hundreds of thousands of people worldwide, there is question of survival, due to the pandemic.

The corona era has greatly impacted the way businesspeople used to interact with. A firm handshake, impressive gait, eye contact, a warm welcome, all these make a meeting momentous. But, alas! The Corona Pandemic has made the world a low-touch economy, i.e., meeting sans any goodies of gesture and posture. And the woes do not end here—its implications have trickle-down effect, it percolates deeper and deeper. It has changed the very basic fabric of influencing a person.

You cannot exchange your visiting cards, (you might be thinking that you have a choice of sending your cards through WhatsApp, but I am sure, you will drop this idea before meeting that person!) You cannot put your booklet so that the person you are going to meet could create an account of impression about you and think favourably of what products you sell, or the services that you offer.

So, what is the way out? Is there any silver lining in these clouds? Is there something that creates magical effect? And the answer is Book. Book is arguably the only way you can use as a weapon to win the world. Those who are authority in their respective fields, will always be followed and looked upon; this time even more, because today an authority is needed more than any time.

So, how you can become authority? You can become authority by authoring a book. As simple as that. Always remember, author is authority. Everybody wants to do business with authority. If you become an authority (with a book to your credit), you will become the obvious choice for your targeted readers. You will be heard with rapt attention, you will be perceived as something super special, your words will be likes quotes. And if you happen to be an Entrepreneurs, speakers, coach, consultant, trainer, etc., what more could you ask for?

Just to begin with, I will suggest you Insta book. Some of you might be thinking about an e-book, but it is effective not more than 60%. If you want to create an impressive impact (say, 90%), go for the Insta Book, and do the e-book version of insta-book too. This duo will be so powerful.

- Author tag before your name will create better perception about you.

- You will create Dream Business and inspire others to live better lives.

- Thousands of leads will be there for your business. Your book will become perfect way for capturing leads.

- You will no longer remain as Underpaid, Underestimated, and Undervalued.

- You will be qualified to Charge Higher.

- You will be perceived as an Expert.

- Writing book will stamp your authority. You will become an Authority. You will become a Prominent Figure in your Field.

- You will stand away from the crowd.

- Book helps you expand your own network by creating a good story, for example a passion project. Passion project books are written for selfless purposes. The writer of a passion project simply wants to share his or her knowledge, experience, and research about a certain issue because he or she truly wants to enlighten others about a cause or topic. Chandan Goyal, Author of "How to Manufacture Time", Dr. Roopinder Dogra, Author of Prisms of Life, and Ram Pujari, Author of Ek Aur Damini are few of our passion project authors.

- To Grow your Network

  A book is a great way to connect with influential people in your industry—authors, journalists, podcasters, and bloggers—who can grow your network in some amazing ways.

Asootosh Kkant, Author of Club 3.0 built lots of connections with top-notch clubs through this book. He has now more clients than his highest expectations. Now, he is writing his second book— "Be A Power Connector."

- To Share your Story

  The future of business will be the story. In this Low Touch Economy, you need something unique to you. And the story is that unique element that can change the game for you, even if you are an

Entrepreneur, Speaker, Coach, Consultant. So, many of us out there have some stories to tell. Whether it's a biographical tale of triumph, a step-by-step guide to solving a problem, or a fictional story crafted to directly impact decisions making parts of your Clients/Prospects' brains. No matter what your story is, you can always use it to make a difference in people's lives. You have all these beautiful ideas running wild in your head. It's indeed not fair for you to keep something so great, trapped inside—the best way to remain alive in the minds of your clients and prospects.

I know the title of the book is Top 10 Reasons, but I cannot stop myself sharing some more reasons.

Let's begin:

- Great revenue generator for your business
- It will build your reputation. Mind, having no reputation at all is just as bad as having a bad reputation
- Book to your credit will gain credibility in your field or create creativity in a new field. Book will help you explain how you could emerge as a successful and worthy of conversing with such a large number of people

- Your book becomes like a Mover & Shaker in your business

- Your book works as your physical presence on the desk, bag, shelf, etc. of your audience. The book makes them think of you, reminds about you and drive them to contact you

- Book is a great way to connect with influencers like authors, journalists, podcasters and bloggers, who are competent enough to grow your network. Resultantly, it saves your time on networking events

- Having best-seller in your name will create magnetism for you; people will keep on getting connected with you almost naturally

- If you have just entered in a particular field or planning to enter, then it will help to make the playing field even between you and the experienced ones, making you respectable from the start

- The last and most important reason is, "Because you always had a desire to write." But, your desire remained suppressed in the absence of a coach, who could have made the journey of book publishing smooth.

- Heavyweight champion business card

  Gone are the days when business persons would start meeting with the people they have an appointment with, after giving their visiting cards. Nowadays, insta-books/books are given in advance so that a particular organisation, company could get a miniature picture of the concerned businessman/woman.

  No doubt insta-books/books of today are the sure-fire way for client attraction, brand building. Simply put, it is the most effective marketing tool of today.

- Preserve legacy for generations

  Books are great way to make your thought outlive you. You can preserve legacy for generations, if you choose to be a writer and pen down your thought, your values, your principles, your dream and what you expect your younger generations to follow. Your generations will preserve it like a holy book. Preserving book for centuries is no longer an uphill task, thanks to the revolution in print technology and online availability of books.

  I always give context to my clients that it's time to leave the game of being Undervalued, Underpaid, and Underestimated. Show the world your Magnetism.

YOUR BOOK IN THE HANDS OF POTENTIAL CLIENTS

Publishing with BestsellerWithDinesh.com is just a child's play. There is huge team of experts taking care of the busiest and the brightest people of society. We have helped a number of such people become a published and distinguished author, and the next one could be you.

The tech-based tools that we use, make our authors' presence felt far and wide and that too within very short amount of time. We take care of each and every thing that is required to make the writing of our authors Known to the World.

Send your insta-book to your Potential Clients or Existing Customers in less than 7 days (including idea thinking, writing, designing and publishing) with completely guided publishing service, which gives you the opportunity to see your book getting ready for publishing in front of your eyes without disturbing your daily routine.

Your 3 to 16 hours are more than sufficient

LET'S MEET OVER A CUP OF COFFEE

I am excited to see you write and publish your first book! Imagine the people who will be inspired by your book. Imagine the solutions that you'll provide through your book.

Imagine sharing your story and lifting people through your words. Imagine making a difference to someone else's life. Isn't that what life is all about?

Write your book for the right reasons. Write your book from the perspective of someone, who wants to give value to its readers. Write your book with pure intentions.

As you give, you get so much more in return. This is the real formula to succeed! Give and you will receive.

If you are a business owner, write a book about how your products and services could provide solutions to your customers' problems. Inspire people.

If you're a speaker and you want to reach out to more companies and audience, imagine how much your book could duplicate you and speak on your behalf to thousands of people, one at a time. And you know what? One speech can get you invitation to many other speeches. You can sell from stage even when organiser not allowing it. We can provide you powerful methods of doing it. Many speakers leave huge business on platter by not selling anything when they speak in an event.

In my journey so far as a publisher, I have come to know that there are good number of people who very much appreciate the idea of book writing, but they somewhat drop the idea, because they think that they lack the ideas required to create a book and business around it.

I have also decided to do something substantial for the Entrepreneurs, Intrapreneurs, Speakers, Coaches and Consultants who are the real heroes of our society and the true nation builders, for I do not want them to remain undervalued, underestimated and underpaid. Apart from this reason, one thing that keeps me motivated is the glittering eyes of my published authors and their success stories with the book published with Pendown Press. How they were commanding the Course of Conversation while dealing with their potential clients and how they cracked the deal on their terms, how they used JVM(Joint Virtual Machine) to generate leads from the unknown circle, when they wore CAP...used Circle Activation Protocol to get business from nearby networks, so on and so forth.

It will not be a hyperbole if I say that I have dedicated my life, right through my student years in making the best products and giving the best services to the people, who listen to me and trust me. But, again... it's my Dharma.

YES, if I fail to make you aware about the services I am offering, it would be crime and you will end up buying inferior quality products/availing superficial services.

I am not worried about the money wasted on buying inferior quality products. More than the money being wasted on having these products or/and services, time and brand that you lose is my real concern. The time that will be wasted procuring these products or services and the brand that you missed, will never be earned back. And I want to protect you from that. If you want to experience the First Tool of MM Methodology (Marketing Magnetism Methodology), get the idea of Insta-book Writing, planning and publishing strategy, all that you need to do is to make yourself available for just 15 minutes. Yes, you have read it RIGHT! Remedies for all these deficiencies are now just 15 minutes away.

To Book your slot you can also WhatsApp at

📞+91 8130886000

Wishing You World Class Book

Dinesh Verma
Your Publisher Friend

TESTIMONIALS

It would be injustice if I would not acknowledge Dinesh's Strategic Book Planning.

It has actually made my book Bestseller as a result of that I have become an authority in my niche.

Dr. Ridwana Sanam
Author of "How to write off your pain?"

Dinesh's teaching and constant support were a great blessing for me! He not only helped me write my first book but also got it published.

What I am today is all because of Dinesh.

Dr. S. Veda Padma Priya
Author of "Life, Survival and Beyond"

Dinesh altered my Perspective about book writing. He never treats book as another commodity. For him and – it's transformational tool. If you want to be a successful author, trust me, you got to seek Dinesh's guidance. Period.

Mukesh Kulothia
Author of "Move Mountains"

I used to chase clients in many networking events. When I met Dinesh. I got convinced within 15 minutes of conversation to publish my first ever book and that too relevant to my target clients. That was one of the best decisions I took for my business growth.

Vinod K. Pandita
Author of "The Powerful CEO"